WALT DISNEY'S MICKEY MOUSE ADVENTURES

TAKE-ALONG COMIC

GEMSTONE PUBLISHING

TIMONIUM, MARYLAND

STEPHEN A. GEPPI
*President/Publisher and
Chief Executive Officer*

JOHN K. SNYDER JR.
Chief Administrative Officer

STAFF

LEONARD (JOHN) CLARK
Editor-in-Chief

GARY LEACH
Art Director

SUSAN DAIGLE-LEACH
Production Manager

MELISSA BOWERSOX
Director-Creative Projects

• IN THIS ISSUE •

Mickey Mouse
MOUSE ON THE LAM
Story: Pat & Carol McGreal Art: Joaquin

Donald Duck
THE MUMMY
Story: Rune Meikle Art: Fecchi
Dialogue: Gary Leach

Original interior color by **Egmont**
Color modifications by **Susan Daigle-Leach**
Lettering by **Gary Leach** and **Susan Daigle-Leach**

Mickey Mouse
THE IDOL OF THE SCAREDIES
Story: Bruno Sarda Art: Massimo De Vita
Dialogue: Lance Caselman
Lettering: Gary Leach

Cover art by Pat Block • Cover color by Gary Leach

**ADVERTISING/
MARKETING**

J.C. VAUGHN
Executive Editor

ARNOLD T. BLUMBERG
Editor

BRENDA BUSICK
Creative Director

JAMIE DAVID
Executive Liaison

SARA ORTT
Assistant Executive Liaison
Toll Free
(888) 375-9800 Ext. 410
ads@gemstonepub.com

MARK HUESMAN
Production Assistant

MIKE WILBUR
Shipping Manager

**WALT DISNEY'S
MICKEY MOUSE
ADVENTURES 1**

Take-Along Comic
August, 2004

Published by
Gemstone Publishing

MICKEY MOUSE

MOUSE on the LAM

NEXT EVENING, AT A A POSH RESTAURANT...

THIS IS SUCH *FUN*, MICKEY! TELL ME, DO YOU LIKE MY NEW SHOES? THEY WERE *VERY* EXPENSIVE!

BUT I *HAD* TO HAVE THEM ONCE I HEARD WE WERE *DINING ELEGANT!*

HM? OH...YEAH, THEY'RE *SWELL*, MINNIE!

MICKEY MOUSE! IT'S OBVIOUS YOU *COULDN'T* CARE LESS! LET'S CHANGE THE SUBJECT, THEN!

SORRY...

IT LOOKS LIKE THAT NEW STATE-OF-THE-ART LASARIUM THEATER COMPLEX IS DUE TO OPEN ANY DAY NOW! THAT'S EXCITING, ISN'T IT?

EXCITING?!

I'LL TELL YOU HOW I FEEL ABOUT THAT *FUTURISTIC FARCE!* I *HATE* IT!!

??!

WHY DO PEOPLE NEED LASER-LIGHTSHOWS, ANYWAY? CAN'T THEY JUST PLAY TIDDLEY-WINKS OR MUMBLEDY-PEG LIKE IN THE OLD DAYS?!

THAT PLACE IS AN *EYESORE!* WORSE! IT'S A *MENACE!* IT'LL CAUSE CONGESTIONS! TRAFFIC JAMS! HEALTH HAZARDS!

MICKEY?

I CAN'T *STAND* THE SIGHT OF IT! *GRRR...* IF IT WAS REDUCED TO A SMOKING PILE OF *RUBBLE,* I'D BE A HAPPY MOUSE!!

MICKEY!!!

YOU'RE *SCARING* ME! *WHAT'S* COME OVER YOU?

I...I...SHEESH... I DON'T KNOW...

C'MON, MINNIE! I'LL DROP YOU OFF AT YOUR HOUSE AND GO HOME! I THINK *I* NEED A GOOD NIGHT'S SLEEP!

LATER THAT NIGHT, A NOISE ROUSES MINNIE...

GASP! SOMEONE'S IN THE HOUSE... RIGHT HERE IN THE *BEDROOM!*

EEEEK!!

MICKEY! WHAT'RE YOU *DOING?!*

...HUH?!

AW, *NO!* NOT *AGAIN!*

WHY IN HEAVEN'S NAME ARE YOU *TAKING* MY NEW SHOES?!

HEH...GUESS I'VE BEEN HAVING A *SLEEP-WALKING* PROBLEM LATELY...

WELL, YOU JUST MARCH HOME TO YOUR *OWN* BED AND *STAY* THERE!

LATER THAT NIGHT...

GRAND OPENING TOMORROW

...THE NEW LASARIUM THEATER STANDS READY TO OPEN ITS DOORS TO THE PUBLIC! ALL IS QUIET...

...WHEN SUDDENLY...

BAAAA-BOOOOOOOOOMMM!!!

GRAND OPENING TOMORROW

NEXT MORNING, AT MICKEY'S HOUSE...

MMMMMFF! WHAS'AT...? SOMEONE AT THE FRONT DOOR..?

KNOCK! KNOCK! KNOCK!

WHY, CHIEF O'HARA! WHAT BRINGS YOU HERE?

UNHAPPY BUSINESS, OLD FRIEND!

I'M AFRAID I'VE GOT TO *ARREST* YOU!

WHAT?!!

CUFF HIM, BOYS!

THIS IS *NUTS!* WHAT ARE YOU CHARGING ME WITH?!

MALICIOUS DESTRUCTION OF PUBLIC PROPERTY! THE NEW LASARIUM WAS *BLOWN TO BITS* LAST NIGHT!

AND YOU THINK *I* DID IT?! THAT'S *RIDICULOUS!*

YOU KNOW ME, CHIEF! I'M A *NICE* GUY! I'D NEVER *DO* SUCH A THING!

NOT MY CALL, MICKEY!

MICKEY'S TRIAL SOON BEGINS...

YOU MAY BE AWARE, MEMBERS OF THE JURY, OF TWO OTHER RECENT EXPLOSIONS, ONE IN FLYSPECK, THE OTHER IN GOOSETOWN, THAT HAVE CAUSED EXTENSIVE DAMAGE TO PUBLIC PROPERTY!

NOW, WE ARE *NOT* HERE TO ESTABLISH WHO WAS BEHIND THOSE INCIDENTS...

...BUT I WOULD LIKE YOU TO KEEP IN MIND THAT ONE THING CAN LEAD TO ANOTHER! I REFER TO THE DEFENDANT'S RECENT *BEHAVIOR!*

ALL RIGHT, MISTER GOOF! CAN YOU DESCRIBE THE DEFENDANT'S CHARACTER?

SURE! MUH PAL MICK'S A *SQUARE* GUY! HE *AIN'T* GOT A CRIMINAL BONE IN HIS BODY!

ISN'T IT A FACT THAT YOU *YOURSELF* CAUGHT HIM BREAKING INTO YOUR HOME?!

WELL...YEAH! BUT I CAN EXPLAIN...

I HAVE *NO* FURTHER QUESTIONS AT THIS TIME! CALL THE NEXT WITNESS!

...BUT...BUT...

AFTER THE BRIEFEST DELIBERATION IN THE CITY'S HISTORY...

MEMBERS OF THE JURY! HAVE YOU REACHED A VERDICT?

WE *HAVE*, YOUR HONOR!

WE FIND THE DEFENDANT — *GUILTY* AS CHARGED!

GULP!

MICKEY MOUSE! FOR YOUR *HEINOUS* CRIME, I SENTENCE YOU TO *TEN* YEARS IN LEAVEMWORST PENITENTIARY!

NO!!

I'VE GOT TO PUT ON THE *LEG-IRONS*, MICKEY!

OH, MICKEY! TELL ME THIS *ISN'T* HAPPENING!

BE BRAVE, MINNIE! THINGS'LL WORK OUT... I *HOPE*!

GAWRSH, MICK! I'LL BAKE YUH *CAKES* AN' SEND 'EM TO YUH IN TH' *SLAMMER!*

YEAH...SURE...THAT'LL BE SWELL, GOOFY...

LET'S GO, SON!

AND SO, OUR HERO HITS THE ROAD TO THE BIG HOUSE...

SO LONG, MICKEY! KEEP YOUR NOSE CLEAN AND *MAYBE* YOU'LL GET TIME OFF FOR GOOD BEHAVIOR!

I'M GOING TO PRISON JUST LIKE...*PETE!* YUCK! WHAT A REVOLTIN' DEVELOPMENT!

SIGH! I KNOW WHAT I SAW ON THE VIDEOTAPE, BUT...I *COULDN'T* HAVE DONE IT! I'M NOT THAT KIND OF MOUSE! BESIDES, I *LIKED* THE IDEA OF A LASARIUM THEATER!

COME TO THINK OF IT, WHAT *HAPPENED* TO THE SILICON CHIP I TOOK OUT OF THAT LASER GIZMO?!

AND HOW DID I GET THE KNOWLEDGE AND TECHNICAL SKILL TO *DISMANTLE* THE DINGUS ANYWAY?!

NO DOUBT ABOUT IT! THERE'S SOMETHING *FISHY* GOING ON! BUT WHAT CAN I *DO* ABOUT IT NOW?!

MAYBE MORE THAN YOU THINK, MICKEY...

THESE GUARDS ARE OUT LIKE LIGHTS... BUT THEY'RE OKAY! AND THIS ONE'S GOT THE *KEYS* TO MY SHACKLES ON HIS BELT!

MAN, *THAT* FEELS BETTER! BUT WHAT DO I DO NOW?!

SHOULD I REMAIN HERE LIKE A GOOD SCOUT UNTIL THE POLICE ARRIVE? OR TAKE THIS CHANCE TO CLEAR MY NAME?!

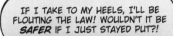

IF I TAKE TO MY HEELS, I'LL BE FLOUTING THE LAW! WOULDN'T IT BE *SAFER* IF I JUST STAYED PUT?!

NAH!

SHORTLY...

...OOOO! IT WAS LIKE A WATER SLIDE...

THE PRISONER'S *GONE*, CHIEF!

AH, MICKEY, OLD FRIEND! *WHAT* HAVE YOU DONE?

YOU LEFT A PATH AS EASY TO READ AS THE FRONT PAGE! I COULD FOLLOW IT IN A NEW YORK MINUTE...

...BUT MAYBE I SHOULD IGNORE IT! THIS COULD BE YOUR ONE CHANCE TO CLEAR YOURSELF!

MY, MY! WHAT A *MESS*!

OUR MAN'S BEEN ON THE RUN FOR NINETY MINUTES, AVERAGE FOOTSPEED OVER UNEVEN GROUND FOUR MILES AN HOUR! GIVES US A SEARCH RADIUS OF SIX MILES!

?!

I WANT A HARD TARGET SEARCH OF EVERY GAS STATION, FARM HOUSE, HEN HOUSE AND *DOG HOUSE* IN THE AREA!

AS FOR YOU LOCAL *YOKELS,* ESTABLISH CHECKPOINTS AT FIFTEEN MILES ALONG EVERY ROAD LEADING FROM THIS SPOT!

YOUR FUGITIVE'S NAME IS MISTER MICKEY MOUSE! GO *GET* 'IM!

WELL! OF ALL THE FLIPPIN' *NERVE!*

MEANWHILE... I'VE WASTED TOO MUCH TIME IN THESE WOODS RUNNING AROUND IN CIRCLES! GOT TO GET TO A ROAD! MAYBE I CAN HITCH A RIDE!

YES! *THIS* IS MORE LIK— UH OH!

WHREEEEEEEOOO

AWP!

ON SECOND THOUGHT, THE WOODS SUIT ME *FINE!*

WAIT! WHAT'S *WITH* YOU GUYS?! HEE HEE HEE! STOP! IT *TICKLES!* GET OFFA ME, YOU BIG LUGS!

WOOF! YARF!

HEY, CAN *I* HELP IT IF DOGS *LIKE* ME?

EVEN THOUGH THESE HOUNDS AREN'T DANGEROUS, THEY'LL *STILL* LEAD THE COPS MY WAY! I'VE GOT TO DITCH 'EM!

YIP?!

GO ON, FELLAHS! FETCH THE STICK!

ARF! WOOF! YAP! YARF!

NOW TO DO A LITTLE *WADING* IN THE STREAM! THOSE CRITTERS CAN'T FOLLOW MY SCENT THROUGH WATER!

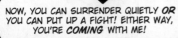

HE'S *GONE!* WHEW! I'M SAFE... FOR THE MOMENT!

BUT I *CAN'T* KEEP THIS UP! IT'S ONLY A MATTER OF TIME BEFORE THAT GUNG-HO G-MAN RUNS ME TO GROUND!

IF I'M EVER GOING TO GET OUT OF THIS JAM, I'VE GOTTA *PROVE* I'M *INNOCENT!*

HMM! THOSE OTHER TWO EXPLOSIONS, IN GOOSETOWN AND FLYSPECK! I'VE GOT TO FIND OUT MORE ABOUT THEM! DETAILS THAT *WEREN'T* PUBLICLY DISCLOSED!

AND WHERE *BETTER* TO FIND DETAILS LIKE THAT THAN IN SEALED POLICE FILES?

THAT NIGHT...

SO THE MEN SPENT THE DAY ON THE RIVER AND TURNED UP *BUPKIS!* SO WHAT?! I'M STILL *CONVINCED* THE CULPRIT IS OUT THERE SOMEWHERE!

IF THAT'S TRUE, MARSHALL...

...PERHAPS YOU SHOULD *BACK OFF!* MICKEY WILL *PROVE* HE'S INNOCENT!

SEZ YOU, CHIEF! HE'S STILL A FUGITIVE!

WE'VE JUST GOTTA FIGURE OUT *WHERE* HE'LL SURFACE! YOU! WHAT ARE YOU DOING?

THINKING, SIR!

WELL, THINK ME UP A FIZZY POP AND A GLAZED DONUT WITH SOME OF THOSE LITTLE SPRINKLES ON TOP! *PRONTO!*

GLEEP!

YES, SIR!! WHOOPS! 'SCUSE ME! I'M HERE TO CLEAN, GENTS! WON'T GET IN TH' WAY, I PROMISE!

I'LL START IN HERE!

HM? FINE! CHIEF! WHERE'S A MAP?! I NEED A *MAP!*

CASE FILES

SO FAR, SO GOOD! NOW LET'S SEE WHAT I CAN DIG UP ON THE GOOSETOWN AND FLYSPECK EXPLOSIONS!

BINGO! *HERE'S* WHAT THE POLICE *DIDN'T* RELEASE TO THE MEDIA! SOME PRETTY ARRESTING STUFF IT IS, TOO!

BOTH EXPLOSIONS COVERED UP *ROBBERIES!* IN GOOSETOWN A CONCAVE MIRROR WAS STOLEN BEFORE THE PLANETARIUM THERE BLEW UP!

AND IN FLYSPECK AN ENERGY AMPLIFIER WENT MISSING FROM THE WRECKAGE OF A DESTROYED PHYSICS LABORATORY!

ADD TO THAT THE SILICON CHIP FROM THE LASARIUM! BUT...*WHAT'S* IT ADD UP *TO?!*

I'LL BE BACK IN A JIFFY, GENTS! FORGOT MY...URM...FLOOR WAX!

GOSH DARN IT! WHERE COULD THAT *FERSHLUGGINER* ESCAPEE BE?!!

OH, I HEAR HE'S A *CLEVER* ONE! WHY, HE COULD BE RIGHT UNDER YOUR *NOSES* AT THIS VERY MOMENT! TA TA!

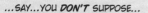

...SAY...YOU *DON'T* SUPPOSE...

MICKEY?!!

STOP THAT CLEANING LADY!!

TOO LATE! HE'S *GONE!*

BUT HE CAME *BACK* TO TOWN! HE'S *AFTER* SOMETHING! WE'VE JUST GOT TO FIGURE OUT HIS NEXT MOVE!

...AUTHORITIES REMAIN *BAFFLED* AS TO THE WHEREABOUTS OF THE DANGEROUS FUGITIVE...

MICKEY! THANK GOODNESS! I WAS SO *WORRIED!*

GEE, MINNIE! IT'S GREAT TO SEE YOU, TOO!

BUT I WOULDN'T HAVE COME HERE IF I DIDN'T NEED YOUR *HELP* IN A BAD WAY!

WHAT CAN I *DO?*

I THOUGHT, MAYBE THERE'S A SITE ON THE INTERNET THAT CAN CLUE ME IN!

TO *WHAT?!*

TO THE SORT OF DEVICE THAT COULD BE ASSEMBLED FROM A STATE-OF-THE-ART SILICON CHIP, A CONCAVE MIRROR, *AND* AN ENERGY AMPLIFIER!

EUREKA! THIS ONE GOT THE ANSWER! THOSE COMPONENTS CAN BE COBBLED TOGETHER TO MAKE A MONSTER *LASER CANNON!*

BUT HOW COULD SUCH A LASER CANNON BE USED? IT'S RANGE WOULD BE SO *WIDE!*

YOU'RE RIGHT! WITH THAT *AMPLIFIER*, ITS SWEEP COULD COVER HUNDREDS OF MILES!

UNLESS...IT WAS OPERATED FROM *SPACE!*

BUT WHO WOULD *WANT* SUCH A THING? AND WHY? TO *CONQUER* THE EARTH?!

WHAT ELSE? AND THAT POINTS TO ONLY *ONE CULPRIT*, MINNIE!!

MICKEY MOUSE! THIS IS *MARSHALL MARSHALL!* COME OUT WITH YOUR HANDS UP!

HOLY CANNOLI! THE GOVERNMENT GUNTZEL! HE'S *TRACKED* ME DOWN!

WHAT DO WE *DO*, MICKEY?!

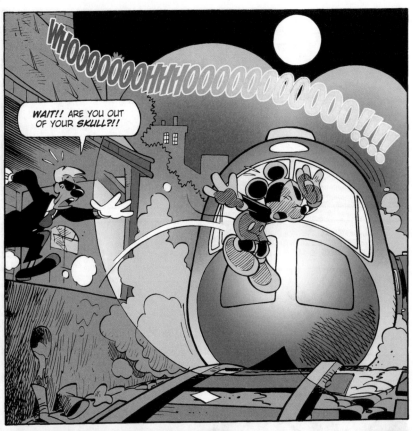

I SHOULD HAVE KNOWN THAT SOONER OR LATER I'D HAVE TO MAKE ONE OF THESE JUMPS FOR *REAL!*

WHA...?!!

CHUGGA-CHUGGA-CHUGGA-CHUGGA!!

BULL'S EYE! THIS IS CERTAINLY A *NEW* WAY OF HOPPING TRAINS!

THUMP!

NO! NO! *NO!* NOT AGAIN! HOW MANY TIMES CAN THIS *ONE PERP* EVADE MY CHASES AND DRAGNETS?!

AS MANY TIMES AS IT *TAKES*, FEDERAL MARSHALL MARSHALL, UNTIL I'VE *CLEARED* MY NAME!

YOUR LUCK WILL *RUN OUT*, MOUSE! I'LL *GET* YOU YET!!

DAWN FINDS MICKEY IN A GRIMY DINER ON *THE OUTSKIRTS OF GOOSETOWN...*

SO WHAT'VE I GOT? A LASER CANNON THAT'S SUPPOSED TO GO INTO EARTH ORBIT! THAT MEANS A ROCKET IS NEEDED TO LAUNCH IT! BUT *WHERE* DO YOU HIDE A ROCKET?!

EAT AT JOE'S

LESSEE...IF I SCRIBE THE TRIANGLE FORMED BY THE THREE CITIES WHERE THE EXPLOSIONS TOOK PLACE...THEN RIGHT HERE, SMACK DAB IN THE MIDDLE IS...

OF *COURSE!* THE ABANDONED SNORAD MISSILE BASE! *PLENTY* OF PLACES THERE TO HIDE – AND LAUNCH – A *ROCKET!*

IF THE CREEP BEHIND THIS IS WHO I *THINK* IT IS, THAT'S *GOT* TO BE WHERE HE'S SET UP HIS HEADQUARTERS!

BUT I *CAN'T* TAKE HIM ON ALL ALONE! BETTER CALL IN THE *RESERVES...*

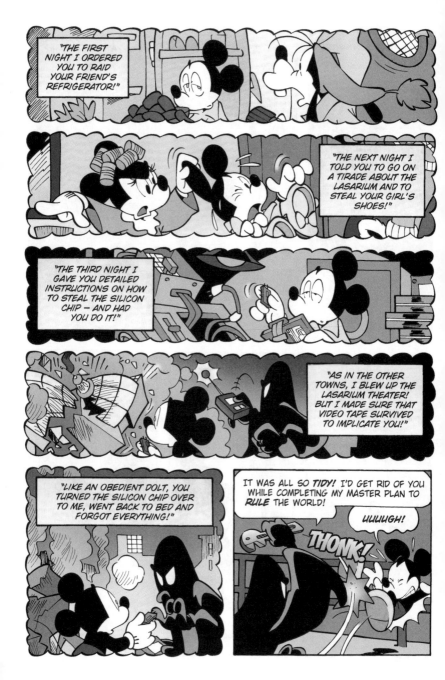

AND IT WILL *STILL* SUCCEED! THE ROCKET'S COUNTDOWN HAS BEGUN!

...OOOOOO...

ALL I HAVE TO DO IS PACK IN THE PAYLOAD — MY LASER CANNON!

NOT IF *I* CAN HELP IT, CHUM!

OOOFF!!

GET OFF ME, YOU IRKSOME *RODENT!*

SMACK!

URF!

I DREAM, I SCHEME, THEN YOU WALTZ IN AND *WRECK* EVERYTHING! WHY I DON'T PUT YOU OUT OF MY MISERY ONCE AND FOR ALL IS...

GACK!

HIYA, MICK! HERE I AM! AND RIGHT ON *TIME*, TOO!

THE JIG'S UP, BLOT!

DO YOU REALLY THINK THAT BIRD-BRAINED BOHUNK CAN *HELP* YOU?!

HE ALREADY *HAS!* TAKE A LOOK!

AWP!

HEY! I WUZ *TAILED* BY THEM TRICKY COPS! I'M SORRY, MICKEY!

OKAY, FUGITIVE! YOU'VE PLAYED OUT YOUR HAND! I HOPE FOR YOUR SAKE YOU'VE TURNED UP SOMETHING *PERSUASIVE!*

YOU BET I HAVE! *HERE'S* YOUR MAN, MARSHALL!

AND *THERE* ARE THE ITEMS HE STOLE FROM THE BUILDINGS HE BLEW UP!

MY SCHEME'S *RUINED*, SO I MIGHT AS WELL FESS UP!

I DID IT ALL! *I* FRAMED THE MOUSE! *I* BUILT A LASER CANNON! *I* MIGHT HAVE RULED THE WORLD! HA*HAHAHAHA!!*

AND SO, BACK IN COURT...

IT IS CLEAR FROM THE NEW EVIDENCE AND THE ATTENDANT TESTIMONY OF FEDERAL MARSHALL MARSHALL THAT THE *PHANTOM BLOT* WAS BEHIND THE CRIMES IN QUESTION! MICKEY MOUSE' CONVICTION IS VACATED, AND ALL ARE CHARGES DROPPED!

YAHOO!

I NEVER DOUBTED YOU FOR A MINUTE, MICKEY! I ALWAYS KNEW YOU WERE *INNOCENT!*

I *COUNTED* ON THAT, CHIEF!

NOT BAD WORK FOR A CIVILIAN! NOW EXCUSE ME, I'VE A *MANHUNT* FOR THE BLOT TO PENCIL INTO MY SCHEDULE!

GOOD LUCK!

SHUCKS, MICK! I STILL FEEL KINDA BAD! LETTIN' TH' LAW *TAIL* ME TUH TH' MISSILE BASE AN' ALL!

HA HA! DON'T YOU *GET* IT, GOOFY?

I KNEW ALL ALONG MARSHALL MARSHALL WOULD FOLLOW YOU THERE! *THAT'S* WHY I CALLED YOU IN THE FIRST PLACE!

GAWRSH! THEN I *WAS* A BIG HELP, AFTER ALL!

OH, MICKEY! I'M SO *GLAD* YOU'VE BEEN CLEARED! EVEN THOUGH IT WAS KIND OF EXCITING HAVING A DANGEROUS *FUGITIVE* FOR A BOYFRIEND!

TO CELEBRATE, I GOT YOU A *PRESENT!* HERE! OPEN IT UP!

FOR *ME?* JEEPERS, YOU *SHOULDN'T* HAVE.

WOW! NEW PAJAMAS WITH CONVICT STRIPES! THANKS, MINNIE! MAYBE WHEN I GO TO BED FROM NOW ON, THESE WILL REMIND ME TO JUST *SLEEP* — AND *FORGET* ABOUT THE WALKING!

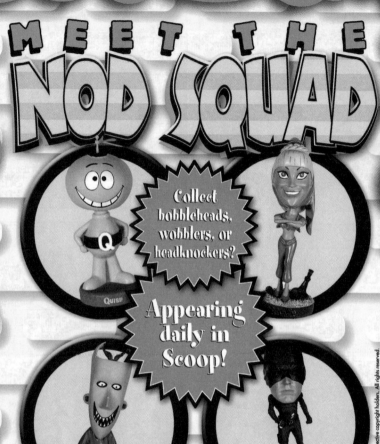

MEET THE NOD SQUAD

Collect bobbleheads, wobblers, or headknockers?

Appearing daily in Scoop!

Daredevil, Jeannie, Spider-Man, the Osbournes, Tony the Tiger, Wonder Woman plus many more of your favorite Yes Men are quaking and quivering through the electronic pages of Scoop. Crammed with earth-shaking character images and the latest industry news, Scoop is the FREE, weekly, e-newsletter from Gemstone Publishing and Diamond International Galleries for collectors and pop culture enthusiasts of all ages. Just visit http://scoop.diamondgalleries.com to check it all out and subscribe. So remember, if you're lacking vital Bobblehead information - don't get the Bobblehead blues, just log onto Scoop for the hottest Bobblehead news!

SCOOP THIS JOINT IS JUMPIN'!

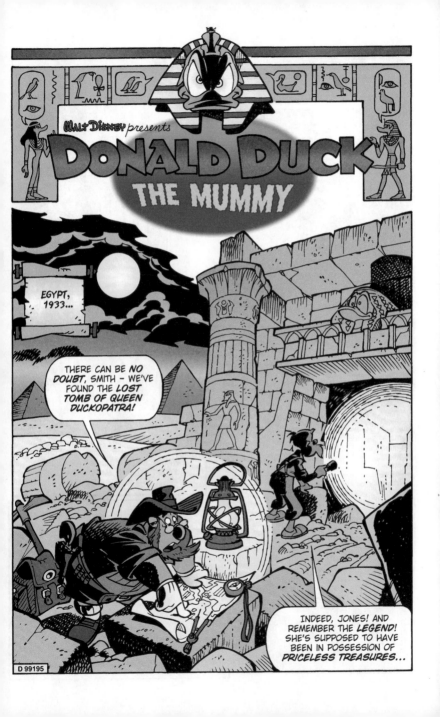

OH?

YOU!

LISTEN UP, YOU OLD *TIGHTWAD!* THIS IS THE *HOUR OF RECKONING!*

YOU'VE ALWAYS HAD ME SLAVING AT *YOUR* WHIM – ON CALL 24-7!

NOW I'M CALLING ON YOU FOR AN *ADVANCE* ON MY SALARY – *RIGHT THIS MINUTE!*

SURE!

IS HE *FEELING* ALL RIGHT?

...BUT SOON SHE'LL **TELL** ME WHERE IT IS — ONCE I'VE **REVIVED** HER! AND FOR THAT...

...I HAVE THIS — THE **REVIVIFIER 3000**! IT'S DESIGNED TO DELIVER **INTENSE RESUSCITATING ENERGY** TO ANYTHING STRAPPED INTO IT!

IF **THIS** CONTRAPTION CAN'T **KICKSTART** THAT MUMMY, NOTHING CAN!

HOWEVER, I CAN'T RUN THE RISK OF **DAMAGING** THE MUMMY, SO I NEED TO CONDUCT A **TRIAL RUN** WITH A **TEST SUBJECT**...

...AND IF THERE'S ANYONE WHO NEEDS A GOOD **STIMULATING JOLT**, IT'S YOU, NEPHEW!

ME?!

LOOK INTO THE *VAPOR* AND TELL ME WHAT YOU SEE!

I SEE THE UNIVERSAL SIGN OF *VICTORY*...

...BUT I ALSO SEE MY BELOVED *DUCKOPATRA IN TEARS!* WHY DOES SHE WEEP?

MAYBE IT'S TEARS OF *JOY—HUH?*

HE'S COMING AROUND!

HOLY COW! I WAS A *REAL PRINCE* BACK THERE IN *ANCIENT EGYPT!*

INTERESTING, BUT INCONCLUSIVE! NOW PIPE DOWN WHILE I SET UP A *SECOND TEST RUN!*

AND *YOU* WERE EXCHANGING SWEET NOTHINGS WITH THAT...

...THAT *POMPOUS BIMBO!* HOW *DARE* YOU, YOU *TWO-TIMER!*

THAT'S *ANOTHER* PROBLEM WITH ROMANCE – TOO DING-BLASTED *NOISY!*

LOOK WHAT'S *HAPPENED!*

HUH? THE *FLOORBOARD'S* BROKEN OFF AND REVEALED A *HIDDEN PLATE...*

...WITH AN *INSCRIPTION* ON IT IN ANCIENT *HIEROGLYPHS!*

WHAT DOES IT SAY?

DONALD! I SHOULD'VE KNOWN IT WAS *YOU* TANGLED UP IN THAT! AT LEAST YOUR GOOFING CAME IN *HANDY* FOR ONCE!

SPEAKING OF *MUMMIES* – WHERE'D YOU PUT *MY* MUMMY?

NUMBSKULL! YOU'VE PUT IT IN FRONT OF A SOUVENIR SHOP! I CAN'T TELL *WHICH ONE* IT IS!

SOUVEN

SALE! MUMMIES!

HMM...I THINK I KNOW HOW TO SINGLE OUT *MY* MUMMY! *DAISY,* GIVE DONALD A *BIG KISS!*

???

WELL, THERE'S CERTAINLY NO HARM IN DOING *THAT!*

DON'T BET ON IT!

FLUMF

AH, *THERE* SHE IS!

HOW DID YOU KNOW?

THE MUMMY *REACTS* EACH TIME YOU SHOW DONALD *AFFECTION!*

BY THE WAY, YOU'D BETTER WATCH OU–

CRACK

SEE? NOW LET'S FIND THAT *PYRAMID!*

OKAY, OL' PAL! RECOGNIZE *THIS?*

?...!!

C'MON, OL' PAL, SHOW US WHERE *THIS* IS, OKAY?

DUCKOPATRA! I'D RECOGNIZE THAT ENIGMATIC EXPRESSION ANYWHERE!

HEY!

BUT STILL NO *PYRAMID!* MAYBE YOU DIDN'T ASK THAT DUMB DROMEDARY THE *RIGHT* QUESTION, AFTER ALL!

THAT *GREEDY* BEAST! MY SOUVENIR FOR THE *BOYS!*

AND *WHERE* DOES HE THINK HE'S GOING NOW?

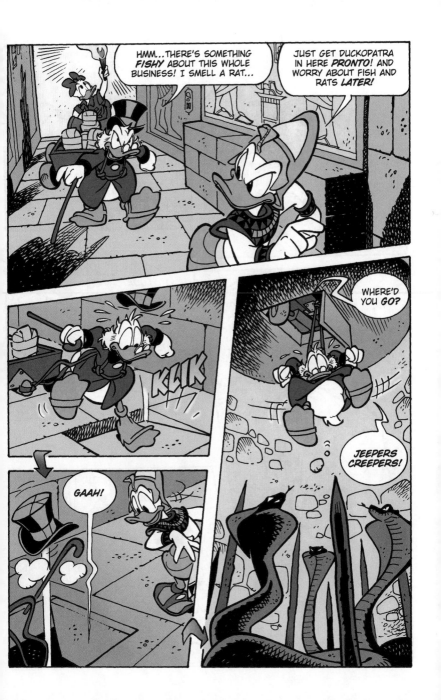

"SO I DECIDED TO JOIN YOU IN THAT LATER AGE! I HAD THIS SPECIAL PYRAMID BUILT FOR MY RESURRECTION, AND MAGICON PUT ME INTO A DEATHLIKE SLEEP, ARRANGING TO HAVE ME INTERRED AS BEFIT MY ROYAL PERSONAGE!"

DRATTED *BANDAGES!*

IT WAS RISKY, BUT WORTH IT! *NOW* WE'RE TOGETHER ONCE MORE, MY LOVE!

GLURF!

SNORT! KEEP AWAY FROM *MY DONALD,* YOU CHEAP FLOOZY!

AFTER *6000 YEARS* I'M NOT AS *FIT* AS I USED TO BE, BUT...

...I CAN STILL *HANDLE* AN ATTACKER WITH BUT THE MEREST *FLICK OF A FINGER!*

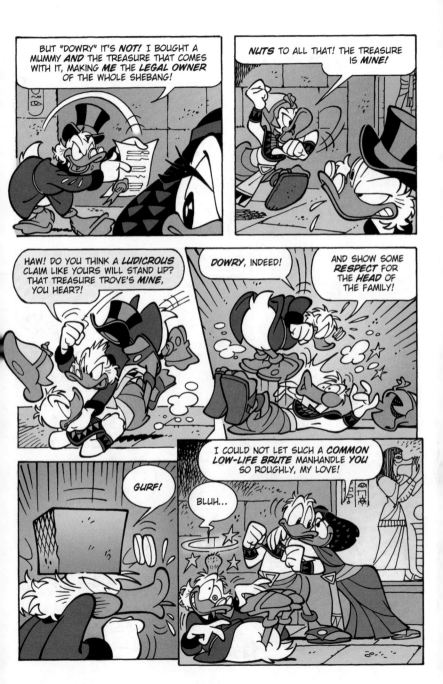

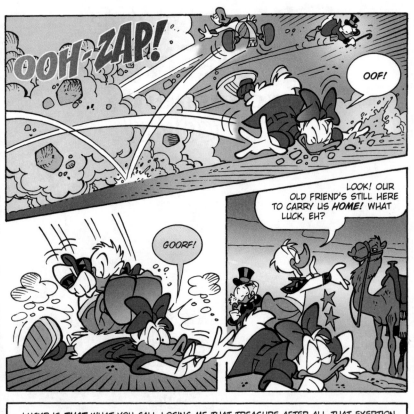

OOH-ZAP!

OOF!

LOOK! OUR OLD FRIEND'S STILL HERE TO CARRY US *HOME!* WHAT LUCK, EH?

GOORF!

LUCK? IS *THAT* WHAT YOU CALL LOSING ME THAT TREASURE AFTER ALL THAT EXERTION AND EXPENSE? I'VE A GOOD MIND TO *BILL YOU* FOR THE ENTIRE EXPEDITION!

AND WHAT'S THE IDEA *LANDING* RIGHT ON TOP OF ME, YOU *CLUMSY OAF?*

SIGH! SUCH IS MY *PRESENT* LIFE...

OH-OH! THE PLANE FROM BANGKOK HAS ALREADY LANDED!

WELL, A TOUGH GUY LIKE *ARIZONA DIPP* WON'T MIND BEING ALONE FOR A BIT!

GASP! S-S-SPIDER! B-BIG SPIDER...!

IT'S JUST A *TOY*, MISTER!

PUT THAT THING *AWAY!* HERE, STUFF IT IN THIS BOX, QUICK!

NO...NOT IN *THAT* ONE!

YOWP!

ARIZONA, WHAT'S GOING ON?

MICKEY! BOY, AM I GLAD *YOU'RE* HERE!

THAT B-BULLY WAS T-TERRORIZING ME WITH LETHAL, INFERNAL OBJECTS!

C'MON, ARE YOU JOKING? THAT LITTLE KID? *TERRORIZING* A TOUGH HOMBRE LIKE YOU? THAT'S JUST SILLY!

WHEN YOU SAID YOUR LAST ADVENTURE GOT TO YOU, I DIDN'T THINK YOU MEANT TO THIS EXTE–

YIKES!!

SIGH...HAVE YOU *NO* SHAME?

NOPE...

HIS COURAGE RESERVES ARE BONE DRY! THE ONLY CURE...

BZZ-Z-Z

...IS PROGRESSIVE TRAUMA THERAPY – TO GRADUALLY EXPOSE HIM TO EVER GREATER PERILS!

ARMED WITH THE DIAGNOSIS...

A COUPLE WEEKS RELAXING AT MY PLACE AND YOU'LL BE BACK TO YOUR ABNORMAL SELF!

GULP!

AAAAAH! M-MONSTER!

YOUR BACKYARD IS FULL OF GIGANTIC, RAVENOUS WORMS! UH...

WHAT IS IT?

WOULD YOU LEAVE THE LIGHT ON?

THE NEXT DAY, MICKEY TRIES TO ACCUSTOM HIS FRIEND TO DANGER, BUT...

NOOO! NOT THE ROLLER COASTER!

Tickets

...ARIZONA PROVES TO BE A DIFFICULT PATIENT...

C'MON, JUST ONE MORE STEP THERE!

I...I CAN'T! D-D-DIZZY!

AND WHAT IF A *BLOOD-THIRSTY WORM* GOES FOR MY THROAT?

THIS IS THE REGION WHERE THE SCAREDIES LIVED!

GULP! THOSE MOUNTAINS LOOK LIKE *SWISS CHEESE!*

SWAMP

ACCORDING TO LEGEND, THE IDOL IS IN ONE OF THOSE CAVES!

IF IT EXISTS!

THAT'S A CHANCE WE GOTTA TAKE! THAT IDOL IS MY ONLY HOPE!

ALL RIGHT, ARIZONA! LET'S BUY OUR PLANE TICKETS!

HEE HEE! NOW I KNOW YOUR *SECRET*, ARIZONA DIPP!

I'LL GET THE IDOL FIRST AND HE'LL BE STUCK BEING *ARIZONA CHICKEN* FOREVER!

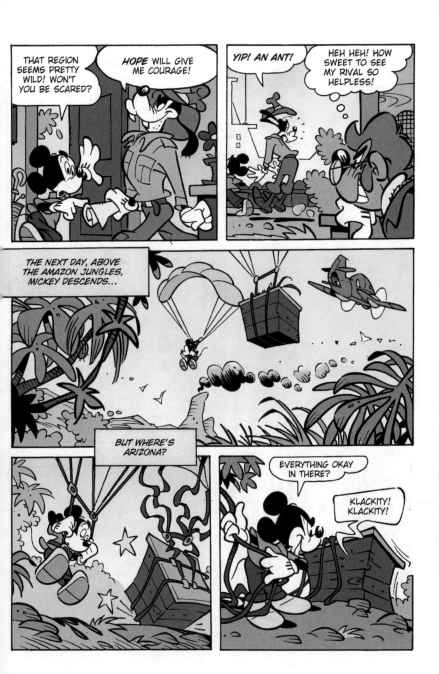

YOU BRING YOUR *MARACAS* ALONG?

N-NO...KLAK KLAK...IT'S JUST MY CHATTERING TEETH!

THERE WERE NO EGG ROLLS IN THERE! YOU *TRICKED* ME!

NO CHOICE! YOU COULDN'T HAVE *PARA-CHUTED* ON YOUR OWN.

IT'S THE *ONLY WAY* DOWN HERE! THERE'S NO PLACE FOR AN AIRPLANE TO LAND IN THIS JUNGLE!

WE'LL PROCEED ON FOOT FROM HERE...

...WHEN YOUR KNEES STOP *KNOCKING!*

S-SORRY...

WAAH!

WHAT THE – ?!

A *COBRA!* A DOUBLE-FANGED *LEAPING* COBRA!

ITS BITE IS EQUAL TO A *THOUSAND...*

...*NORMAL* SNAKES!

ZOMP

WOW! WHAT A *LEAP!*

PHEW! YOU SURE GOTTA WATCH YOUR *STEP* AROUND THESE PARTS!

A-AND NOT JUST ON THE *GROUND!*

!

AAIIEE!!

RUN!

ZOW

AND SO AM *I!* HEH, HEH, HEH!

LOOK, A CLAY POT!

GOOD! THE LOST CITY MUST BE CLOSE!

IT WON'T BE EASY TO *FIND* IT!

THE JUNGLE HAS OVERGROWN JUST ABOUT EVERYTHING AROUND HERE...

HOW ABOUT *THIS* STONE?

MMM...HERE'S MORE! PAVING STONES, BY THE LOOK OF 'EM!

LET'S CLEAR ALL THE BRUSH, MICKEY! MAYBE THIS IS *IT!*

GULP! *ALL* THE BRUSH?!

IT LOOKS LIKE A GIANT *CHESSBOARD!*

NEXT YOU'LL WANT TO PROVE THAT THEY'RE...

...THE *INVENTORS* OF CHESS!

MAYBE THEY *WERE!*

MAYBE *PEOPLE* WERE THE PLAYING PIECES! KNIGHT TO C2! HOP!

OR MAYBE THEY USED STATUES LIKE THIS...NOPE, DOESN'T BUDGE!

THEN WHAT *IS* ITS PURPOSE?

DUNNO! THAT PICTOGRAPH OF A SETTING SUN...HMM, WHAT'S *THAT* MEAN, I WONDER?

LOOK! THE SUN IS SETTING RIGHT NOW...

...AND THE STATUE CASTS A SHADOW THAT POINTS...

HERE! THAT'S IT! THE IDOL MUST BE UNDER THIS STONE!

THE LEGEND MENTIONED A *CAVE*...

YEAH, BUT YOU CAN'T ALWAYS *TRUST* LEGENDS! BELIEVE ME...

"...*I KNOW ALL ABOUT THESE THINGS!*"

PHEW! NOTHING!

HMPH! WELL, AS THE FELLER SAYS, SOMETIMES A *SHADOW* IS JUST A *SHADOW!*

SOON ENOUGH...

WAIT UP...DON'T FORGET YOUR *COURAGE DEPLETION!* LET ME GO IN FIRST!

WHAT DANGER COULD THERE BE?

WELL, THERE ARE *JAGUARS* IN THE AREA...

YEAH, YEAH...

EEYAAH!!

I KNEW IT! IT'S A *JAGUAR'S* DEN!

N-NO...JUST A *BAT* CAVE! BRRR!

FLAP FLAP

GIVE ME THE FLASHLIGHT! I'LL GO FIRST!